Discover the

VIOLIN

CW00531510

Huge Hits

Editorial, production and recording: Artemis Music Limited • Published 2004

IMP

International MUSIC Publications

Introduction

Welcome to DISCOVER THE LEAD, part of an instrumental series that provides beginners of all ages with fun, alternative material to increase their repertoire, but overall, enjoyment of their instrument!

For those of you just starting out, the idea of solo playing may sound rather daunting.
DISCOVER THE LEAD will help you develop reading and playing skills, while increasing your confidence as a soloist.

You will find that the eight well-known songs have been carefully selected and arranged at an easy level - although interesting and musically satisfying. You will also notice that the arrangements can be used along with all the instruments in the series – flute, clarinet, alto saxophone, tenor saxophone, trumpet, violin and piano – making group playing possible!

The professionally recorded backing CD allows you to hear each song in two different ways:

- a complete demonstration performance with solo + backing
- backing only, so you can play along and DISCOVER THE LEAD!

Wherever possible we have simplified the more tricky rhythms and melodies, but if you are in any doubt listen to the complete performance tracks and follow the style of the players. Also, we have kept marks of expression to a minimum, but feel free to experiment with these – but above all, have fun!

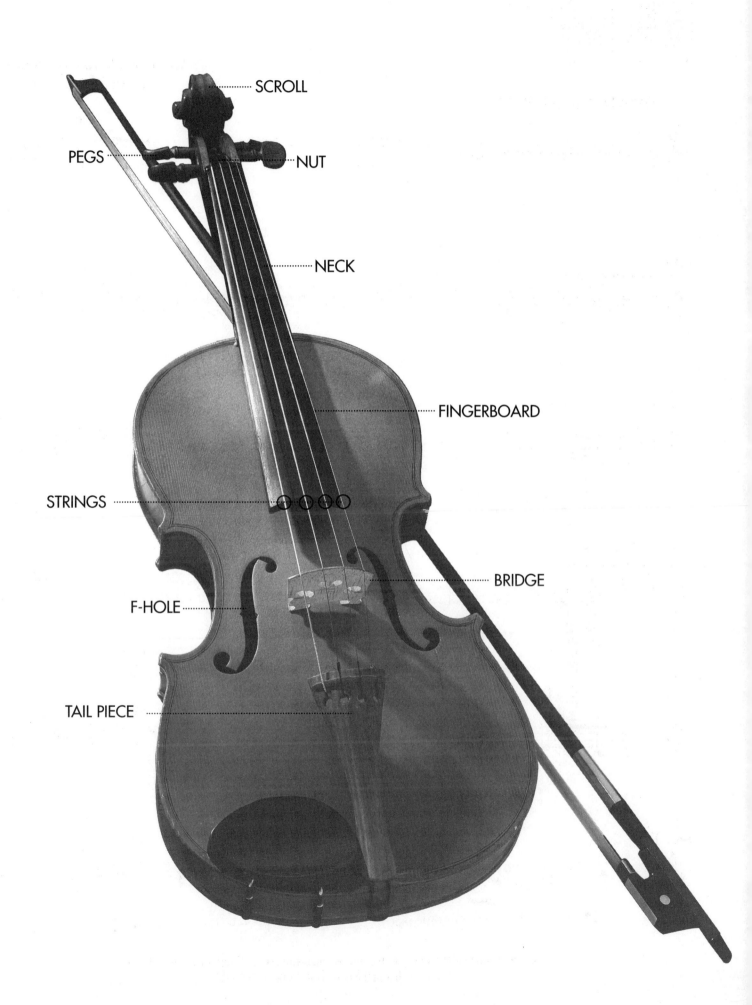

SCROLL

PEGS

NUT

NECK

FINGERBOARD

STRINGS

BRIDGE

F-HOLE

TAIL PIECE

Are You Ready For Love?

Demonstration

Backing

Words and Music by Thomas Bell,
Leroy Bell and James Casey

Moderate pop tempo

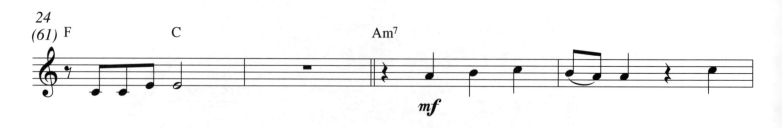

Crashed The Wedding

Demonstration   Backing

Words and Music by
James Bourne and Tom Fletcher

Crazy In Love

Demonstration   Backing

Words and Music by Eugene Record,
Beyoncé Knowles, Rich Harrison and Shawn Carter

Moderate pop tempo

Hole In The Head

Demonstration   Backing

Words and Music by
Brian Higgins, Miranda Cooper,
Timothy Powell, Nick Coler, Niara Scarlett,
Keisha Buchanan, Mutya Buena and Heidi Range

Brightly

Whatever your instrument is...
you can now

TAKE THE LEAD *PLUS*

- Available in C, Bb, Eb and Bass Clef editions, this new concept opens up Take The Lead to a wider range of instruments, including cello, trombone, bassoon and baritone saxophone

- Flexible arrangements allowing players to team up with any number of instruments able to read from one of the 4 editions – C, Bb, Eb and Bass Clef

- Each edition contains the full instrumental score in either 2,3 or 4 parts

- Professionally recorded backing tracks that re-create the sound of the original recordings

TAKE THE LEAD

- Each book comes with a professionally recorded CD containing full backing tracks for you to play along with, and demonstration tracks to help you learn the songs

- Ideal for solo or ensemble use - in each edition, songs are in the same concert pitch key

- Each book includes carefully selected and edited top line arrangements; chord symbols in concert pitch for use by piano or guitar

- Suitable for intermediate players
  "A great way to get some relaxing playing done in between the serious stuff" **Sheet Music Magazine**

Discover The Lead

- This 'spin off' of the Take The Lead series is ideal for beginners of all ages, grades 1-3

- The books contain simplified arrangements of well-known tunes to help the beginner develop reading and playing skills, while increasing confidence as a soloist

- Includes a useful fingering chart plus a CD with full backing and demonstration tracks

- Lots of helpful hints and technical tips to help you get to know your instrument

SHARE THE LEAD

- All pieces have been carefully selected and arranged at an easy level to provide fun material for today's instrumentalists

- All the arrangments work not only as duets for one particular instrument, but with all other instruments in the series (i.e. the flute book works with the clarinet book)

- The professionally recorded CD allows you to hear each song in 4 different ways – a complete demonstration of the track; part two plus backing so you can play along on part one; part one plus backing so you can play along on part two; and the backing only so you and a friend can Share The Lead!

Take The Lead

90s Hits
Air That I Breathe – I'll Be There For You – Something About The Way You Look Tonight – Frozen – How Do I Live – Angels – My Heart Will Go On – I Don't Want To Miss A Thing

Movie Hits
Because You Loved Me – Blue Monday – (Everything I Do) I Do It For You – I Don't Want To Miss A Thing – I Will Always Love You – Star Wars – The Wind Beneath My Wings – You Can Leave Your Hat On

TV Themes
Coronation Street – I'll Be There For You (Theme from Friends) – Match Of The Day – (Meet) The Flintstones – Men Behaving Badly – Peak Practice – The Simpsons – The X-Files

The Blues Brothers
She Caught The Katy And Left Me A Mule To Ride – Gimme Some Lovin' – Shake A Tail Feather – Everybody Needs Somebody To Love – The Old Landmark – Think – Minnie The Moocher – Sweet Home Chicago

Christmas Songs
Winter Wonderland – Little Donkey – Frosty The Snowman – Rudolph The Red Nosed Reindeer – Christmas Song (Chestnuts Roasting On An Open Fire) – Have Yourself A Merry Little Christmas – Santa Claus Is Comin' To Town – Sleigh Ride

Swing
Chattanooga Choo Choo – Choo Choo Ch'Boogie – I've Got A Gal In Kalamazoo – In The Mood – It Don't Mean A Thing (If It Ain't Got That Swing) – Jersey Bounce – Pennsylvania 6-5000 – A String Of Pearls

Jazz
Birdland – Desafinado – Don't Get Around Much Anymore – Fascinating Rhythm – Misty – My Funny Valentine – One O'Clock Jump – Summertime

Latin
Bailamos – Cherry Pink And Apple Blossom White – Desafinado – Guantanamera – La Bamba – La Isla Bonita – Oye Mi Canto (Hear My Voice) – Soul Limbo

Number One Hits
Believe, Cher – Careless Whisper, George Michael – Dancing Queen, Abba – Flying Without Wings, Westlife – I Will Always Love You, Whitney Houston – Livin' La Vida Loca, Ricky Martin – When You Say Nothing At All, Ronan Keating – You Needed Me, Boyzone

Classical Collection
Sheep May Safely Graze (Bach) – Symphony No. 40 in G Minor, 1st Movement (Mozart) – The Toreador's Song from Carmen (Bizet) – Hall Of The Mountain King from Peer Gynt (Grieg) – Radetzky March (Strauss) – Dance Of The Sugar Plum Fairy from The Nutcracker (Tchaikovsky) – Polovtsian Dances from Prince Igor (Borodin) – The Swan from Carnival of the Animals (Saint-Säens)

Rock 'n' Roll
Be–Bop–A–Lula – Blue Suede Shoes – Blueberry Hill – C'mon Everybody – Great Balls Of Fire – The Green Door – Jailhouse Rock – Let's Twist Again

Ballads
Amazed – Get Here – I Don't Want To Miss A Thing – A Little Bit More – My Heart Will Go On – The Rose – Swear It Again – The Wind Beneath My Wings

British Isles Folk Songs
All Through The Night – Greensleeves – The Leaving Of Liverpool – Loch Lomond – Men Of Harlech – Scarborough Fair – The Skye Boat Song – When Irish Eyes Are Smiling

Musicals
Fame – Food Glorious Food – If I Were A Rich Man – Over The Rainbow – Send In The Clowns – Singin' In The Rain – Tomorrow – Wouldn't It Be Lovely

Smash Hits
I'm Like A Bird – It's Raining Men – Lady Marmalade – Out Of Reach – There You'll Be – Uptown Girl – The Way To Your Love – Whole Again

Grease
Beauty School Dropout – Greased Lightnin' – It's Raining On Prom Night – Look At Me, I'm Sandra Dee – Summer Nights – There Are Worse Things I Could Do – We Go Together – You're The One That I Want

Huge Hits
Anything Is Possible – Come Away With Me – Come Undone – Cry Me A River – Hero – On The Horizon – Sound Of The Underground – Spirit In The Sky

Take The Lead Plus

Pop Hits
Can't Fight The Moonlight – Can't Get You Out Of My Head – Eternity – Fallin' – Handbags And Gladrags – I Want Love – It's Raining Men – What If

Jazz Standards
Do Nothin' 'Till You Hear From Me – It Don't Mean A Thing (If It Ain't Got That Swing) – Jeepers Creepers – Misty – Moonlight In Vermont – On Green Dolphin Street – Stardust – The Shadow Of Your Smile

Share The Lead

Chart Hits
Dancing Queen – Flying Without Wings – How Do I Live – Love's Got A Hold On My Heart – My Heart Will Go On – More Than Words – When You Say Nothing At All – You Needed Me

Film & TV Hits
Beautiful Stranger – Charlie's Angels – Don't Say You Love Me – I Believe – I'll Be There For You – Pure Shores – Searchin' My Soul – When You Say Nothing At All

Discover The Lead

Chart Hits
All The Things She Said – Can't Nobody – Feel – I'm With You – No Good Advice – Rock Your Body – Say Goodbye – Sorry Seems To Be The Hardest Word

Huge Hits
Are You Ready For Love – Crashed The Wedding – Crazy In Love – Hole In The Head – I'm Your Man – Jump (For My Love) – Mandy – Superstar

Pop Hits
Don't Tell Me – Genie In A Bottle – Holler – Life Is A Rollercoaster – Millennium – Reach – Say What You Want – Seasons In The Sun

Classical Collection
Air On A G String (Bach) – Ave Maria (Schubert) – La Donna E Mobile from Rigoletto (Verdi) – Largo from New World Symphony (Dvořák) – Lullaby from Wiegenlied (Brahms) – Morning from Peer Gynt (Grieg) – Ode To Joy from Symphony No. 9 (Beethoven) – Spring from The Four Seasons (Vivaldi)

Christmas Carols
Away In A Manger – The First Nowell – Hark! The Herald Angels Sing – O Come All Ye Faithful – O Little Town Of Bethlehem – Once In Royal David's City – Silent Night – We Three Kings Of Orient Are

Kids' Film & TV Themes
Animaniacs Theme – Can We Fix It? – Chitty Chitty Bang Bang – Hedwig's Theme – Number One – Over The Rainbow – Pokemon Main Theme – Scooby Doo Theme

Smash Hits
Anything Is Possible – Bop Bop Baby – Hero – Hey Baby – How You Remind Me – It's OK – Just A Little – One Step Closer

Whatever your instrument is...
you can now

TAKE, DISCOVER & SHARE

Available for Violin
7240A TTL Swing
7177A TTL Jazz
7084A TTL The Blues Brothers
7025A TTL Christmas Songs
7006A TTL TV Themes
6912A TTL Movie Hits
6728A TTL 90s Hits
7263A TTL Latin
7313A TTL Number One Hits
7508A TTL Classical Collection
7715A TTL Rock 'n' Roll
8487A TTL Ballads
9068A TTL British Isles Folk Songs
9245A TTL Musicals
9406A TTL Smash Hits
9656A TTL Grease
9891A TTL Huge Hits
7287A STL Chart Hits
8493A STL Film & TV Hits
8856A DTL Pop
9165A DTL Classical Collection
9306A DTL Christmas Carols
9566A DTL Kids' Film & TV Themes
9731A DTL Smash Hits
9916A DTL Chart Hits
10014A DTL Huge Hits

Available for Clarinet
7173A TTL Jazz
7236A TTL Swing
7080A TTL The Blues Brothers
7023A TTL Christmas Songs
7004A TTL TV Themes
6909A TTL Movie Hits
6726A TTL 90s Hits
7260A TTL Latin
7309A TTL Number One Hits
7505A TTL Classical Collection
7711A TTL Rock 'n' Roll
8483A TTL Ballads
9064A TTL British Isles Folk Songs
9241A TTL Musicals
9402A TTL Smash Hits
9652A TTL Grease
9893A TTL Huge Hits
7285A STL Chart Hits
8491A STL Film & TV Hits
8852A DTL Pop
9161A DTL Classical Collection
9302A DTL Christmas Carols
9562A DTL Kids' Film & TV Themes
9727A DTL Smash Hits
9918A DTL Chart Hits
10016A DTL Huge Hits

Available for Drums
7179A TTL Jazz
7027A TTL Christmas Songs

Available for Trumpet
7083A TTL The Blues Brothers
7239A TTL Swing
7176A TTL Jazz
7262A TTL Latin
7312A TTL Number One Hits
7503A TTL Christmas Songs
7507A TTL Classical Collection
7714A TTL Rock 'n' Roll
8486A TTL Ballads
9067A TTL British Isles Folk Songs
9244A TTL Musicals
9405A TTL Smash Hits
9655A TTL Grease
9894A TTL Huge Hits
8494A STL Film & TV Hits
8855A DTL Pop
9164A DTL Classical Collection
9305A DTL Christmas Carols
9565A DTL Kids' Film & TV Themes
9730A DTL Smash Hits
9919A DTL Chart Hits
10017A DTL Huge Hits

Available for Tenor Saxophone
6911A TTL Movie Hits
7238A TTL Swing
7175A TTL Jazz
7082A TTL The Blues Brothers
7311A TTL Number One Hits
7637A TTL Christmas Songs
7713A TTL Rock 'n' Roll
8485A TTL Ballads
9066A TTL British Isles Folk Songs
9243A TTL Musicals
9404A TTL Smash Hits
9654A TTL Grease
9896A TTL Huge Hits
9163A DTL Classical Collection
8854A DTL Pop
9304A DTL Christmas Carols
9564A DTL Kids' Film & TV Themes
9729A DTL Smash Hits
9921A DTL Chart Hits
10019A DTL Huge Hits

Available for Piano
7178A TTL Jazz
7026A TTL Christmas Songs
7364A TTL Latin
7441A TTL Number One Hits
7509A TTL Classical Collection
7716A TTL Rock 'n' Roll
8488A TTL Ballads
9069A TTL British Isles Folk Songs
9246A TTL Musicals
9407A TTL Smash Hits
9657A TTL Grease
9890A TTL Huge Hits
8857A DTL Pop
9166A DTL Classical Collection
9307A DTL Christmas Carols
9567A DTL Kids' Film & TV Themes
9732A DTL Smash Hits
9915A DTL Chart Hits
10013A DTL Huge Hits

Available for Flute
6725A TTL 90s Hits
7079A TTL The Blues Brothers
7235A TTL Swing
7172A TTL Jazz
7022A TTL Christmas Songs
7003A TTL TV Themes
6908A TTL Movie Hits
7259A TTL Latin
7310A TTL Number One Hits
7504A TTL Classical Collection
7710A TTL Rock 'n' Roll
8482A TTL Ballads
9063A TTL British Isles Folk Songs
9240A TTL Musicals
9401A TTL Smash Hits
9651A TTL Grease
9892A TTL Huge Hits
7284A STL Chart Hits
8490A STL Film & TV Hits
8851A DTL Pop
9160A DTL Classical Collection
9301A DTL Christmas Carols
9561A DTL Kids' Film & TV Themes
9726A DTL Smash Hits
9917A DTL Chart Hits
10015A DTL Huge Hits

Available For Recorder
9922A DTL Chart Hits
10020A DTL Huge Hits

Available for Alto Saxophone
7005A TTL TV Themes
7237A TTL Swing
7174A TTL Jazz
7081A TTL The Blues Brothers
7024A TTL Christmas Songs
6910A TTL Movie Hits
6727A TTL 90s Hits
7261A TTL Latin
7308A TTL Number One Hits
7506A TTL Classical Collection
7712A TTL Rock 'n' Roll
8484A TTL Ballads
9065A TTL British Isles Folk Songs
9242A TTL Musicals
9403A TTL Smash Hits
9653A TTL Grease
9895A TTL Huge Hits
7286A STL Chart Hits
8492A STL Film & TV Hits
8853A DTL Pop
9162A DTL Classical Collection
9303A DTL Christmas Carols
9563A DTL Kids' Film & TV Themes
9728A DTL Smash Hits
9920A DTL Chart hits
10018A DTL Huge Hits

Available for C Instruments
9685A TTL Plus Pop Hits
9771A TTL Plus Jazz Standards

Available for Bb Instruments
9686A TTL Plus Pop Hits
9772A TTL Plus Jazz Standards (Brass)
9773A TTL Plus Jazz Standards (Woodwind)

Available for Eb Instruments
9687A TTL Plus Pop Hits
9774A TTL Plus Jazz Standards (Brass)
9775A TTL Plus Jazz Standards (Woodwind)

Available for Bass Clef Instruments
9692A TTL Plus Pop Hits
9792A TTL Plus Jazz Standards

Teachers' Pack
9793A TTL Plus Jazz Standards

Published by:

IMP

International MUSIC Publications

International Music Publications Ltd
Griffin House
161 Hammersmith Road
London
England W6 8BS

Registered In England No. 2703274
Warner Music Group A Time Warner Company

I'm Your Man

Words and Music by
George Michael

Demonstration   Backing

Jump (For My Love)

Demonstration

Backing

Words and Music by Gary Skardina,
Stephen Mitchell and Marti Sharron

Medium pop tempo

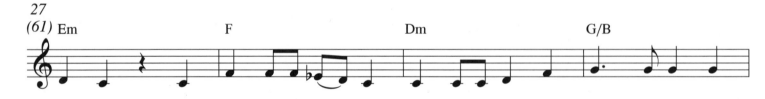

Mandy

Demonstration

Backing

Words and Music by
Richard Kerr and Scott English

Superstar

Words and Music by Mich Hansen,
Joseph Belmaati and Mikkel Sigvardt

Demonstration

Backing

Steady pop tempo

A Guide to Notation

Note and Rest Values

This chart shows the most commonly used note values and rests.

Name of note (UK)	Semibreve	Minim	Crotchet	Quaver	Semiquaver
Name of note (USA)	Whole note	Half note	Quarter note	Eighth note	Sixteenth note
Note symbol	o	♩	♩	♪	♪
Rest symbol	▬	▬	⌡	⌐	⌐
Value per beats	4	2	1	1/2	1/4

Repeat Bars

When you come to a double dotted bar, you should repeat the music between the beginning of the piece and the repeat mark.

When you come to a repeat bar you should play again the music that is between the two dotted bars.

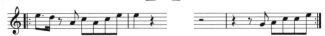

First, second and third endings

The first time through you should play the first ending until you see the repeat bar. Play the music again and skip the first time ending to play the second time ending, and so on.

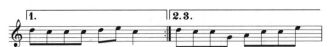

D.C. (Da Capo)

When you come to this sign you should return to the beginning of the piece.

D.C. al Fine

When this sign appears, go back to the beginning and play through to the *Fine* ending marked. When playing a *D.C. al Fine*, you should ignore all repeat bars and first time endings.

D.S. (Dal Segno)

Go back to the 𝄋 sign.

D.S. al Fine

Go to the sign 𝄋 and play the ending labelled *(Fine)*.

D.S. al Coda

Repeat the music from the 𝄋 sign until the ⊕ or *To Coda* signs, and then go to the coda sign. Again, when playing through a *D. 𝄋 al Coda*, ignore all repeats and don't play the first time ending.

Accidentals

Flat ♭ - When a note has a flat sign before it, it should be played a semi tone lower.

Sharp ♯ - When a note has a sharp sign before it, it should be played a semi tone higher.

Natural ♮ - When a note has a natural sign before it, it usually indicates that a previous flat or sharp has been cancelled and that it should be played at its actual pitch.

Bar Numbers

Bar numbers are used as a method of identification, usually as a point of reference in rehearsal. A bar may have more than one number if it is repeated within a piece.

Pause Sign

A pause is most commonly used to indicate that a note/chord should be extended in length at the player's discretion. It may also indicate a period of silence or the end of a piece.

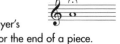

Dynamic Markings

Dynamic markings show the volume at which certain notes or passages of music should be played. For example

pp	= very quiet	*mf*	= moderately loud
p	= quiet	*f*	= loud
mp	= moderately quiet	*ff*	= very loud

Time Signatures

Time signatures indicate the value of the notes and the number of beats in each bar.

The top number shows the number of beats in the bar and the bottom number shows the value of the note.